D0323842

AMAZON PARROTS
KW-012

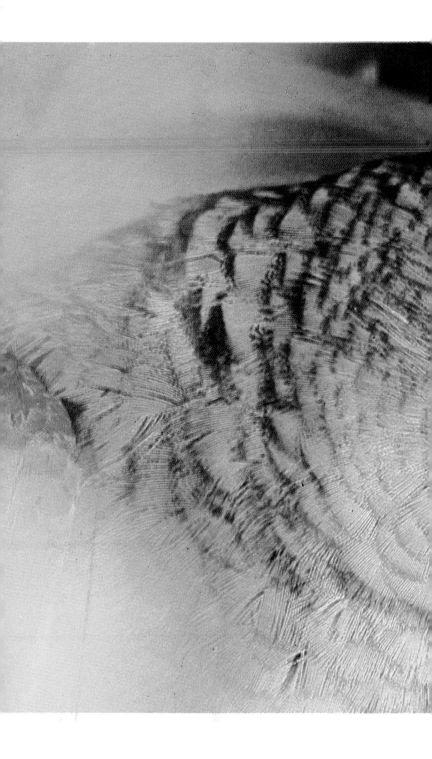

Contents

Overleaf: Yellow-crowned Amazon. **Title page:** Cuban Amazon. **Back endpapers:** Yellow-billed Amazon.

Photographers: American Museum of Natural History, Dr. Herbert R. Axelrod, Tom Caravaglia, Fred Harris, Max Mills, A.J. Mobbs, Dr. E.J. Mulawka, Vince Serbin, Louise van der Meid, Vogelpark Walsrode, Dr. Matthew Vriends.

Distributed in the UNITED STATES by T.F.H. Publications, Inc., One T.F.H. Plaza, Neptune City, NJ 07753; in CANADA to the Pet Trade by H & L Pet Supplies Inc., 27 Kingston Crescent, Kitchener, Ontario N2B 2T6; Rolf C. Hagen Ltd., 3225 Sartelon Street, Montreal 382 Quebec; in CANADA to the Book Trade by Macmillan of Canada (A Division of Canada Publishing Corporation), 164 Commander Boulevard, Agincourt, Ontario M1S 3C7; in ENGLAND by T.F.H. Publications Limited, Cliveden House/Priors Way/Bray, Maidenhead, Berkshire SL6 2HP, England; in AUSTRALIA AND THE SOUTH PACIFIC by T.F.H. (Australia) Pty. Ltd., Box 149, Brookvale 2100 N.S.W., Australia; in NEW ZEALAND by Ross Haines & Son, Ltd., 18 Monmouth Street, Grey Lynn, Auckland 2, New Zealand; in SINGAPORE AND MALAYSIA by MPH Distributors (S) Pte., Ltd., 601 Sims Drive, #03/07/21, Singapore 1438; in the PHILIPPINES by Bio-Research, 5 Lippay Street, San Lorenzo Village, Makati Rizal; in SOUTH AFRICA by Multipet Pty. Ltd., 30 Turners Avenue, Durban 4001. Published by T.F.H. Publications, Inc. Manufactured in the United States of America by T.F.H. Publications, Inc.

AMAZON PARROTS

PAUL R. PARADISE

A History of Bird-Keeping

In her book *Bird-Keeping and Birdcages: A History*, the author, Sonia Roberts, suggests that caged birds are the first true pets that man ever had. She may be correct in making this assumption, since caged birds generally served no utilitarian purpose, whereas dogs and cats were used for other purposes, such as for hunting, pest control and later for food and skins. What is important is that very early in his civilization man went to the trouble to build cages to house birdlife for purposes that were strictly pleasurable and esthetic. No other animal kept by man at this time served this purpose exclusively.

The Chinese may have been the first bird-keepers, though there is no documented evidence of this. The Chinese did selectively breed pheasants at a time when Europeans had yet to discover the wheel. The first recorded keeping of birds and other exotic wildlife goes back to 1500 B.C., when Queen Hatshepsut of Egypt financed an expedition to find

One of the earliest parrots to be discovered was the Cuban Amazon. This illustration is taken from W.T. Greene's book Parrots in Captivity. *This book is highly recommended if you are serious about acquiring knowledge of parrots. Originally published in three volumes in the 1880's, it has recently been reprinted with magnificent color plates and is available at most pet shops which sell birds.*

A History of Bird-Keeping

animals for the royal zoo. Many of the animals kept by the royalty of Egypt, such as crocodiles, falcons and hawks, presumably became deities. Parrots were unknown at this time; the Egyptians did not have a hieroglyph for them.

Documents dated as far back as 600 B.C. show that the Chinese were using cormorants for catching fish; this was considerably before Aristotle, who is credited as being the first Western writer about birds. The practice of using cormorants (family Phalacrocoracidae) still goes on today. Cormorants are sea birds that dive into the water and catch fish. They are very skilled in this due to their long necks. By placing a thread around the neck tight enough so that the cormorants can not swallow their fish, the fisherman is able to fish without using a net or pole. Incidentally, although Aristotle is credited with being the first European to write about birds, Edward Boosey, a well-known ornithologist, claims that approximately one century earlier, in the fifth century B.C., a Greek named Ctesias

wrote about a bird that talked. This bird came from India, according to Ctesias. Aristotle wrote about a bird that he named Psittace, which is the basis for the scientific name used for parrots today.

Tracking down the first birdcage would be impossible and, in any case, probably useless, since the first cages were undoubtedly made of wood slats with a wood bottom. They are more than likely lost to history. Nevertheless, very elaborate aviaries sprang up in the days of the Roman Empire. At this time the keeping of caged birds, especially talking parrots, was considered a mark of status, and the price of such birds often exceeded the price of a slave. One extremely rich Roman, who was one of the pioneers of the mass-produced heating systems used in Roman cities, built a gigantic aviary that matches those produced today. It housed several hundred birds and, instead of metal or wood bars, had hemp netting.

The introduction of birds, especially parrots, into the Western World can be traced

The Amazon parrot is a New World bird which inhabits South America, Mexico, and several of the Caribbean Islands.

primarily to Alexander the Great, who was well known as a bird fancier. When he reached India, he had the peacocks he saw transported home, and he was so enthralled by their beauty that he later issued a decree forbidding the slaughtering of the birds. In the issuing of this decree he may have been influenced by the Indians themselves, who elevated peacocks and parrots to a degree of reverence for their beauty and their talking ability, respectively. Alexander the Great also introduced the Alexandrine parrakeet (*Psittacula eupatria*) to Europe. This bird is named appropriately enough for its transporter, and during the days of the Roman Empire was the most popular caged bird. Another bird brought back by Alexander the Great was the plumhead parrakeet (*Psittacula cyanocephala*).

Panama yellow-fronted Amazon.

The keeping of birds did not become popular among the lower classes until the Industrial Revolution. The building of modern-size zoos was instrumental in exhibiting birds to the public. At one time the London Zoo, built in 1828, had just about every parrot species. The London Zoo was built after the Vienna Zoo (1752) and the Paris Zoo (1793).

Many traveling shows with trick birds were extremely popular in Great Britain during the early 1800's. One of the most famous was Wombell's Menageries, which had talking parrots and performing canaries in costume. Another, formed by a man named John Austin, gave a performance at Buckingham Palace in 1833 before the young lady who would in a few years become Queen Victoria.

In 1894 the Avicultural Society was founded in England, the first of its kind. Similar bird societies were founded in the United States in 1927 and in Australia in 1928. The rise of the bird societies also saw the introduction of a circuit of bird shows. These shows were more accurately bird markets, with different classes based on the quality of the stock. All birds shown at these bird shows were available for purchase afterwards. Today, of course, birds are judged in a variety of categories based solely on esthetic qualities.

Black-billed Jamaican Amazon.

Introduction

There are about 330 species in the family Psittacidae, the parrot family. All 330 species are rightly called parrots, although many of them usually are referred to by other names: macaws, parrotlets, grass parakeets, conures, lories and lorikeets, etc. Members of the parrot family are distinguished by their large hooked beaks, which are rounded. The upper mandible is movable, giving parrots' beaks sufficient force to crack nuts and hard-shelled fruits. Parrots have fleshy tongues. Their feet are adapted to forest life and habitation in trees. They have two toes in front and two behind, and most parrots—especially the Amazons—are agile climbers.

The family contains six subfamilies; all share the above listed traits. Of the six subfamilies, the members of the subfamily Psittacinae are the most numerous; they are often referred to as **psittacine** birds, or parrots. In the subfamily Psittacinae are, in addition to the Amazons, parrakeets, conures, parrotlets, lovebirds, grass parrakeets, and other true parrots, like the African grey parrot (*Psittacus erithacus*).

Psittacines are found principally in tropical and subtropical regions. Usually they will be found in low-lying arid forest areas, although the Andean parrakeet, *Bolboyhynchus orbygnesius*, is found in the mountains at an altitude of 15,000 feet.

Psittacines are almost entirely vegetarian in diet, although in the cage they may accept meat. They are flock birds and in their native countries often are regarded as pests because of their habit of flying down onto cultivated farmland. Many of the species have been cruelly hunted; several are now extinct. The area comprising the West Indies has been especially hard hit. Since 1492, when Columbus landed in this region, twenty-one bird species have become extinct, and of these 13 were members of the parrot family. (These figures are from an article by Tom Marshall in the February, 1977 issue of *American Cage-Bird Magazine*).

Today, many of the Amazon parrots are in danger of becoming extinct, and

A pair of yellow-faced Amazon parrots. Amazons are members of the Psittacidae *family.*

Above: *A yellow-naped Amazon.* **Opposite:** *A yellow-fronted Amazon.*

special emphasis has been placed on endangered species of Amazons in this book. These birds are, of course, no longer available commercially, but the extinction of a species of animal affects us all. The Carolina parrakeet (*Conuropsis carolinensis*) was the only native species of parrot found in the United States. This bird, though once very numerous, went the

A lilac-crowned Amazon. This bird is owned by Lindsay Salathiel of Newport Beach, California.

same way as the passenger pigeon did; the last known specimen died on February 21, 1918 at the Cincinnati Zoo.

Many of the psittacines are well-known talkers. In fact, the most well-known of the talking birds are psittacines. The African grey has the reputation of being the world's greatest talking bird. Recently, the *Guinness Book of World Records* gave the title of world champion talking bird to an African grey named "Prudle," which had a vocabulary of 1,000 words.

Many of the Amazon parrots are excellent talking birds and come very close to the talking ability of the African grey. The difference is in the quality of the voice; Amazons' are more nasal than the African grey's. The Mexican double yellow-head and the yellow-naped Amazon are perhaps the best known talkers among the Amazon parrots.

Incidentally, the African grey has quite a history to it. It was well known to the Portuguese sailors who frequented the African Gold Coast. They called it the "jaco," for that is what they

A yellow-crowned Amazon. Due to their dwindling numbers in the wild, many Amazon species are protected under endangered species regulations.

thought its shrieking sounded like. The African grey was kept as a pet by King Henry VIII. Another African grey,

Above left: *Blue-fronted Amazon.*
Above right: *Northern rosella,*
Platycercus venustus. *Rosellas are
more colorful than Amazon parrots but
are less talented as talkers.* **Left:** *Blue-
crowned mealy Amazon.* **Opposite,
upper left:** *Mealy Amazon.* **Opposite,
upper right:** *This bird appears to be
one of the yellow-headed subspecies
of the yellow-crowned Amazon.*
Opposite, lower left: *Festive
Amazon.* **Opposite, lower right:** *Blue-
fronted Amazon.*

kept by a duchess, was later stuffed and is the oldest known stuffed bird in the world. The parrot, named "Effigie," is over 300 years old and sits in a museum in England.

THE GENUS *AMAZONA*
The Amazon parrots belong to the genus *Amazona*, one of the approximately 80 genera in the subfamily Psittacinae. Taxonomists disagree on the exact classification, but most authorities would accept 27 species and over 50 subspecies in the genus *Amazona*.

Amazons can be found throughout the Central and South American countries and many of the neighboring islands. They are best known of all the New World parrots and, with the exception of the African grey, are the most widely kept of the true

An array of Amazon parrots: red-lored Amazon, orange-winged Amazons, blue-fronted Amazons, mealy Amazon.

A blue-fronted Amazon and a yellow-crowned Amazon enjoying some fresh air. One should not, however, take one's bird outdoors without some sort of restraint.

parrots.

Amazons are medium-size parrots and range from 10 to 19 inches in length. They are solid in build and have a basic coloration of green, although red, blue, purple, black and yellow are also to be found.

Amazons have tails that are slightly rounded. The wings are round and very broad, but not very long. Generally, Amazons are expert climbers. They are also excellent talking birds.

Amazons are widely kept in the United States. They are popular in Europe, which has a more established bird fancy than in the United States, but in Europe the African grey is more popular.

Like all other parrots, Amazons are temperamental. They can be highly affectionate, but sometimes they may be very particular about with whom they are affectionate. Sometimes they can be downright nasty to anyone who approaches their cage. They are also noisy birds and will utter shrieks

21

Above: *Photographed in Singapore at the Jurong Bird Park, these Amazons are in excellent condition. Serious bird parks breed rare birds and protect them from extinction. The bird with the solid yellow head is a double yellow-headed Amazon, while the other bird is a young blue-fronted Amazon.* **Opposite:** *Bird expert Ruth Hanessian poses with a tame yellow-naped Amazon.*

that may keep a bird-owner awake throughout the night until the parrot learns to wake with the family. Nonetheless, Amazons are intelligent birds and usually will become good, affectionate pets with good training. There are many instances of Amazons that became so tame that they were left completely at liberty.

Dr. Matthew M. Vriends, a world-renowned ornithologist who spent some time in Brazil studying Amazons, reports that they fly in large flocks and to all appearances mate for life. Instances of Amazons mating in captivity are rare, however. Vriends also reports that these birds will sleep several hundred in the same tree. Incubation is roughly a month, the same as for the African grey.

Many of the Amazons change feather coloration as they grow older. This is especially true of the yellow-headed species like the Mexican double yellow-head. Amazons have their first molt between eight and ten months. In the wild the hen will lay her eggs in the same tree year after year.

It is sad to state, but many of the Amazons are on the endangered species list. It is quite possible that, in addition to the birds mentioned in this book that are no longer available commercially, many others may soon be added to the list.

AMAZON PARROTS SPECIES

The following list contains the common and taxonomic names of the 27 Amazon parrots species.

Yellow-billed or red-throated Amazon (A. collaria)

Cuban Amazon (A. leucocephala)

Hispaniolan or Salle's Amazon (A. ventralis)

White-fronted or spectacled Amazon (A. albifrons)

Yellow-lored Amazon (A. xantholora)

Black-billed Jamaican Amazon (A. agilis)

Puerto Rican or red-fronted Amazon (A. vittata)

Tucuman Amazon (A. tucumana)

Red-spectacled or Pretre's Amazon (A. pretrei)

Green-cheeked Amazon (A. viridigenalis)

Amazon parrots are able to blend so well with foliage that they often escape the notice of naturalists and ornithologists in the field.

Lilac-crowned Amazon (*A. finschi*)

Red-lored or yellow-cheeked Amazon (*A. autumnalis*)

Red-tailed or Brazilian green Amazon (*A. brasiliensis*)

Blue-cheeked or Dufresne's Amazon (*A. dufresniana*)

Festive Amazon (*A. festiva*)

Yellow-faced Amazon (*A. xanthops*)

Yellow-shouldered Amazon (*A. barbadensis*)

Blue-fronted Amazon (*A. aestiva*)

Yellow-crowned Amazon (*A. ochrocephala*)

Orange-winged Amazon (*A. amazonica*)

Scaly-naped or mercenary Amazon (*A. mercenaria*)

Mealy Amazon (*A. farinosa*)

Vinaceous Amazon (*A. vinacea*)

St. Lucia Amazon (*A. versicolor*)

Red-necked Amazon (*A. arausiaca*)

St. Vincent Amazon (*A. guildingii*)

Imperial Amazon (*A. imperialis*)

Left: Panama yellow-fronted Amazon.
Below: *Ruth Hanessian talking to a trained yellow-naped Amazon.*

Amazon Parrots

The species and subspecies described in this section are not—at least presently—on the protected species list. For the sake of clarity, not every subspecies of each species will be listed here, as in most cases the subspecies are very similar to each other.

The only exceptions are the Double yellow-headed Amazon parrot (*A. ochrocephala oratrix*) and the Panama yellow-fronted Amazon parrot (*A. ochrocephala panamensis*), which are both very popular parrots and deserving of

mention. The double yellow-head and the Panama yellow-fronted are both subspecies of the yellow-crowned Amazon parrot (*A. ochrocephala*).

Yellow-crowned Amazon Parrot (*A. ochrocephala*)

Often called the single yellow-headed Amazon parrot, the yellow-crowned Amazon parrot occupies a wide range, from central Mexico as far south as Peru; it sometimes appears even as far north as southern Texas. It has a great reputation, along with the double yellow-head, as a talking bird. Both birds are very popular. In the young the head color is mostly green, with a few patches of yellow. These patches of yellow will become more numerous as the bird grows older and are a distinguishing factor in telling the age of the bird.

Yellow-crowned Amazons, like many other Amazons, utter a variety of shrieks and whistling noises. They are reported to be strong fliers in the wild and capable of flying long distances. In the wild both male and female will sometimes build a nest; this

is odd, as most Amazons choose a hollow in a tree and don't build a nest. Incubation of eggs takes about a month; the usual clutch contains three eggs.

Yellow-crowned parrots are medium-sized, standing from 14 to 15 inches in length. The crown is yellow and the rest of the head green, although the yellow will gradually spread throughout the head. The cere is black and the beak is dark gray. The iris is orange-colored. The feathers of the nape and hind-neck are green and edged with black. In the young the black edging around the feathers is more pronounced.

Double Yellow-headed Amazon Parrot (*A. ochrocephala oratrix*)

Sometimes called Levaillant's Amazon or the Mexican double yellow-head, the double yellow-head stands about 15 inches in length. The color of the iris is orange. The bill of the double yellow-head is more white than that of the yellow-crowned Amazon parrot. In the young the heads are green speckled with yellow, but as the bird grows older the yellow will gradually cover the entire head. This process will continue over 25 years. In the adult the primaries are black and green. The double yellow-head is found mainly in Mexico and Belize.

Panama Yellow-fronted Amazon Parrot (A. ochrocephala panamensis)

Very similar to the double yellow-head Amazon parrot, this subspecies is about 12 inches in length. The forehead is yellow, with a bluish sheen present; in the young the entire head is green. A patch of red is present at the shoulders. The Panama yellow-fronted parrot is found in northern Colombia and Panama. It is often confused with *A. o. auropalliata*, which is sometimes called the Panama parrot.

Festive Amazon Parrot (A. festiva)

Sometimes called the red-backed Amazon parrot, this subspecies is about 14 inches in length. The general plumage is green. The feathers of the neck are faintly edged with black. The crown has a slight bluish

A yellow-naped Amazon on a typical parrot stand. These stands are enjoyed by almost all parrots and are available at pet shops.

tinge. At the base of the feathers a yellow coloration is present. The iris is yellowish orange.

The red-backed Amazon has a geographical distribution that extends throughout eastern Ecuador, eastern Peru and northwestern Brazil. They

Opposite: *Blue-crowned Amazon.* **Above left:** *Green-cheeked Amazon.* **Above right:** *White-eyed conure.* **Right:** *Salvin's or red-lored Amazon.*

have a loud, brassy shriek and are found close to the water and in the high treetops that line the Amazon River basin. Oddly enough, even though this is one of the more numerous of the Amazons, it is not often seen in captivity. There are no records of its breeding in captivity, nor is any information available concerning its nesting habits.

Dufresne's Amazon Parrot
(*A. dufresniana*)

This parrot is rarely seen in captivity and is described as shy in temperament. According to current reports, this parrot is being driven back in its territory in Brazil, where extensive forest-clearing is taking place.

Dufresne's Amazon parrot, also called the blue-cheeked, has a bluish purple coloration on the cheeks, parts of the neck and ear coverts. The bill is gray, with red at the base of the upper mandible. The general color is dark green. The legs are gray.

Yellow-cheeked Amazon
Parrot (*A. autumnalis*)

This parrot is found throughout the lowlands of eastern and central Mexico and also to Brazil. It flies in flocks that may number from a few individuals to over a hundred. They are very active during the day and feed on a variety of fruits, nuts and berries. The yellow-cheeked, though not often seen in captivity, is very numerous around the Amazon River basin. Though reported to be noisy in the wild, in captivity they tend to be reserved and suspicious. They have been bred in captivity; a lengthy report of a yellow-cheeked's being bred in captivity is given in the book *The Parrots of South America*, by Rosemary Low.

The yellow-cheeked Amazon parrot is 13 1/2 inches in length. It is often called the red-lored Amazon parrot and the scarlet-lored Amazon parrot because of the attractive arrangement of red feathers on the crown.

Green-cheeked Amazon
Parrot (*A. viridigenalis*)

This species is fairly numerous, although found in a limited area in Mexico. Like the yellow-cheeked, the green-cheeked is found in flocks numbering from a few individuals to over a hundred. In flight the birds utter a harsh shriek.

These parrots are great pests and have a reputation for swooping down on cultivated crops, much to the dismay of local farmers. In the wild, these Amazons begin courtship during March. Reportedly, their courtship behavior is accompanied by much shrieking and pecking at each other.

The green-cheeked is about 13 inches in length. It is often called the Mexican red-headed Amazon parrot because of the crimson colors on the forehead, crown and lores. Many people consider this to be the most beautiful of the Amazons. The bill and the iris are yellow. The general plumage is green. In the young the red on the forehead is found only as a patch which gradually expands to cover most of the head. The primaries are blue to black, with a patch of red on the secondaries.

A spectacled Amazon. Members of this species are noted for their aggression toward intruders; they are not shy, as are many other Amazon parrots.

Spectacled Amazon Parrot
(A. albifrons)

This parrot is very common in Mexico and lives in woodlands and dry areas. It feeds on fruits, nuts, berries and leaf buds and is reported to be a pest to farmers; they differ, however, in temperament from other Amazons in being very bold to intruders.

The spectacled Amazon parrot is also called the

white-fronted Amazon parrot, and it is about 14 inches in length. The over-all color of the plumage is green. The forehead and forecrown are white. The crown itself is blue. The feathers of the breast and neck are tinged with black. The size difference between males and females, which is normally slight for parrots, is reported to be very distinct for the spectacled Amazon parrot.

Orange-winged Amazon Parrot (*A. amazonica*)

This parrot occupies a very wide area in northern South America, including parts of Brazil, Venezuela, Colombia and much of Peru. The orange-winged is perhaps the most widely imported Amazon into Europe. It is an excellent talker and makes a good pet. In the United States the Mexican double yellow-head and the yellow-crowned Amazon parrots are more popular. The smaller size of the orange-winged makes it easier to house for bird-keepers.

In the wild orange-winged Amazons are very numerous.

Forshaw reports seeing giant bamboo stems so overladen with them that they were bending under their weight. Haverschmidt, a famous bird naturalist, reports them so common in Surinam that the natives kill them for sport as well as because they are pests. In the wild, orange-wings feast at the top of trees on a variety of fruits, berries and nuts. They utter a variety of shrill shrieks. Their breeding season begins in February and March.

The orange-winged is 13 inches in length. The general plumage is green. There is a very attractive display of orange on the wings, interspersed with black, deep blue and green. The crown is yellow. The iris is orange and the legs pale grey. The beak is a yellowish corn color, but darker at the tip.

Blue-fronted Amazon Parrot (*A. aestiva*)

The blue-fronted Amazon is found throughout Brazil and into Argentina. It is one of the best known of the Amazons and is very popular in Europe. At one time the popularity of this parrot in Great Britain was second only to that of the African grey. The first breeding of the blue-fronted in captivity occurred in 1939. This parrot is an excellent talker.

The blue-fronted mates during March and often has been observed mating in the same nest year after year. Incubation lasts 29 days. Their food is the same as that of most other Amazons: fruits, berries and nuts. In Brazil they are reported to be a farm pest.

The blue-fronted is sometimes mistaken for the orange-winged. The blue-fronted, however, is bigger, standing 14 to 15 inches in length. The forehead is blue. The general plumage is green. The area around the throat, parts of the cheek and around the eyes are yellowish. The iris is orange, and the bill is gray. The primaries are blue and black, with a scattering of red.

A pair of blue-fronted Amazons. These birds are members of two different subspecies.

Cuban Amazon Parrot *(A. leucocephala)*

Found in the mountains and the lowlands of Cuba, the Cuban Amazon has become scarce because of the clearing of the land. It is on the list of endangered species proposed by the Washington Convention of 1975. There are very few individuals in captivity.

The Cuban Amazon parrot is very lively. It is a strong flier and very vocal in flight. The Duke of Bedford reports a strange friendship between a Cuban Amazon and an

Adelaide parrakeet (*Platycercus elegans adelaidae*). Literature on the Cuban is scarce, however.

In the wild, the Cuban Amazon parrot nests in tree hollows, laying three or four eggs; the period of incubation is from 25 to 28 days. The young were reported to spend a further 11 weeks in the nest before leaving.

The plumage is mainly green. The Cuban is 13 inches in length. The back part of the neck is blue. The cheeks, lores and parts of the breast are crimson. The ear coverts are dark gray. The feathers of the upper breast are tinged with black.

Salle's Amazon Parrot (*A. ventralis*)

Salle's Amazon is often called the San Domingo Amazon parrot. It is rarely seen in captivity and is currently on the list of endangered species compiled by the Washington Convention. It is found on the island of Hispaniola and a few other Caribbean islands.

In the wild these parrots nest in holes in trees. Their breeding season is reported to be variable. They are generally seen in pairs or family groups rather than in large flocks. In the air, they are less strong fliers than other Amazons.

Salle's is a small Amazon about 12 inches in length. The over-all plumage is green. The forehead and forecrown are white. A large blackish patch can be observed covering the ear coverts. The beak, legs and feet are flesh-colored. The iris is red. The base of the tail is red. The feathers of the head and mantle are distinctively edged with black.

Yellow-lored Amazon Parrot (*A. xantholora*)

This parrot is found in a limited territory around southeastern Mexico and the Yucatan Peninsula. It has been rarely imported and was recently placed on the list of endangered species by the Washington Convention.

The Yellow-lored Amazon is sometimes thought to be a subspecies of *Amazona albifrons*. Both parrots are markedly similar and in the wild are often found together. Their calls are identical. Early in this century the yellow-lored was reported to be more numerous, but its numbers are dwindling rapidly. It is found in heavy forest areas that make detection difficult.

The general plumage of the yellow-lored is green; the feathers are edged with black. This is a very small parrot, 10 inches in length. The forehead and crown are white, but the blue coloring of the crown, which is present in the spectacled Amazon parrot, is absent in the yellow-lored. The area surrounding the eyes is red. The legs are pale gray. An interesting feature of this parrot is that in the young the forehead is blue, becoming white in the adult.

Lilac-crowned Amazon Parrot (A. finschi)

This parrot also goes by the name Finsch's Amazon parrot. It is not as popular in Europe as it is in the United States, although even in the United States it is not often seen.

The lilac-crowned is found in the mountainous regions of northwestern Mexico at elevations of about 2,000 feet above sea level. This parrot was more numerous at the

The Cuban Amazon is one of the rare Caribbean Amazon species. The South American species are more commonly found in captivity today.

turn of the century, when flocks numbering several hundred in number were often observed. In the wild it feeds on an assortment of fruits, berries and nuts. The species has been bred at the San Diego Zoo. The period of incubation was reported to be 28 days, and the chick was hand-raised for a period of three months.

The general plumage of the lilac-crowned is green, with the feathers edged with black. The forehead is a pale color. The primaries are violet. The iris is orange, the legs greenish gray. The bill is horn-colored. In the young the iris is dark brown. The secondaries are green and blue towards the tip.

Tucuman Amazon Parrot
(*A. tucumana*)

The Tucuman Amazon parrot is rarely seen and today occupies a small area in southeastern Bolivia. It was recently placed on the endangered species list compiled by the Washington Convention of 1975.

The length of the Tucuman is 13 inches. The general plumage is green, with the feathers strongly tinged with black. The forehead is red. The primaries are green, becoming blue towards the tip. The iris is orange-yellow, and the legs are a pale grayish pink.

Red-spectacled Amazon Parrot (*A. pretrei*)

This is a rare parrot in captivity and was placed on the Washington Convention list of endangered birds. Apparently, the red-spectacled was more common in the early part of the century, but widespread clearance of forest land has been largely responsible for its dwindling numbers. Forshaw, however, as recently as 1971, reported that they are quite plentiful in their limited territory in southeastern Brazil. Forshaw reported seeing over a thousand of them in one particular location—but he warns that with the continuing depletion of their natural habitat they will rapidly dwindle in number, as have many of the other Amazons.

The red-spectacled is 13 inches in length. Its forehead is red, as is the area surrounding the eyes and parts of the shoulders. The iris is yellow, and the bill is horn-colored. Parts of the wing feathers are also red. This parrot is very similar to the Tucuman Amazon parrot; they can be distinguished from each other by a patch of red at the wing tips that is found only in the red-spectacled.

Red-tailed Amazon Parrot
(A. brasiliensis)

The red-tailed is also called the Brazilian green Amazon. It is found in a small area in southern Brazil. It once occupied a wider territory, but extensive deforestation in that country has considerably diminished its territory. It has rarely been kept in captivity. In the wild, it is often seen in the company of the red-spectacled Amazon parrot (*A. pretrei*).

The general plumage is green. The top of the head is pinkish. The cheeks, throat and upper breast are grayish, with blue interspersed. The primaries are black and deep blue. The tail has a band of yellow and a band of red. The iris is brown, and the legs are gray.

Vinaceous Amazon Parrot
(A. vinacea)

The vinaceous Amazon is not often seen in captivity; it was placed on the endangered species list proposed by the Washington Convention. The main appearance of the species until this time has been in

A red-lored or yellow-cheeked Amazon parrot.

Europe, where it has a reputation as a colorful Amazon parrot and also a good aviary bird. Although not much has been written about it, the vinaceous is reported to be a very gentle bird, which is not the usual case as far as parrots go. It has been bred in captivity many times. The eggs are oval and smooth. It is found in southeastern Brazil.

The vinaceous is 14 inches

in length. Its over-all plumage is green. The forehead and lores are red. The iris is red, and the legs pale gray. The upper regions of the breast and abdomen are violet, sometimes bluish-green. The primaries are black and blue.

Mercenary Amazon Parrot
(A. mercenaria)

The mercenary Amazon parrot occupies a narrow but extensive coastal area beginning near Venezuela and Colombia and extending south through Bolivia, Peru and Chile. This parrot is very rare, and little information has been published about it. It is considered to be an endangered species.

The mercenary Amazon is a shy bird that occupies hilly, mountainous regions. The natives in the regions in which it lives are rarely able to find its nesting spots. Its call and its nesting habits have thus far not been recorded.

The general plumage is green. The mercenary

Amazon is also called the scaly-naped Amazon and is identified by a yellowish patch on the crown. The iris is red. The legs and the bill are gray. The wings, although green, are laced with red and have black edging.

Yellow-faced Amazon Parrot *(A. xanthops)*

The yellow-faced Amazon, also called the yellow-bellied Amazon, is found mainly in eastern Brazil. It was reported to be more numerous at the turn of the century, but little has been recorded about its habits. Its call is undescribed, and there is no nesting material available.

The over-all plumage is green; some feathers on the nape and hind-neck are edged with dark green and narrowly tipped with black. The iris is yellow. The legs are pale gray. The bill is horn-colored. The primaries and secondaries are edged with a greenish yellow.

A Tucuman Amazon parrot. This rare species can usually only be found in south-eastern Bolivia.

Endangered Amazon Species

From the species descriptions in the foregoing chapter, you can see that many of these species are already quite scarce, and many of them are on the 1975 Washington Convention's list of endangered species. Many of the species in this chapter, in addition to being on the Washington Convention's list, are protected species in their own country and as such have not been available to the public eye for quite some time. It is hoped that a time will come when these species, many of which were numerous at one time, will again become plentiful enough that they can be bought commercially or be on display in zoos across the world.

Puerto Rican Amazon Parrot (A. vittata)

The Puerto Rican Amazon parrot, also called the red-fronted Amazon parrot, is a small and well proportioned parrot. It is about 12 inches long and is found only in Puerto Rico. Forshaw says that a subspecies of *A. vittata* used to exist on a nearby island but is now extinct. The last specimens of this subspecies were collected in 1899.

Dr. Russ, author of *The Speaking Parrot*, reports that the Puerto Rican used to be among the most plentiful of the imported species. Its decline was very rapid at the turn of the century. Reasons for its decline are numerous: hunting for sport, killing as a farm pest and nest-robbing for feathers. Additionally, vast deforestation has helped deplete its numbers. Recently 28,000 acres in the mountain areas of eastern Puerto Rico were set aside as a preserve for the bird.

Surveys made between 1953 and 1956 estimated the number of wild Puerto Rican Amazons as 200; surveys in 1956 estimated their numbers at 50. This number was changed to 30 in 1968, and today only 22 are thought to remain. This parrot is on the Washington Convention's endangered list.

The main color of the Puerto Rican Amazon is

Many rare Amazon species can only be seen in select zoos, while others may only be found in their native habitat.

green, with a narrow band of red on the forehead. Flecks of red also cover the ear-coverts and cheeks. The outer webs of the flight and tail feathers are blue. The tip of the tail is yellow, which is also the color of the bill and the iris.

Senseless predation is not the sole cause for the decline of the Puerto Rican Amazon. During World War II, the cutting down of old Colorado trees contributed to the greatly decreasing numbers of this parrot. Scientists have since learned that this parrot will not nest in any other tree. The Puerto Rican is also vulnerable to attacks by rats and by a bird called the pearly-eyed thrasher (*Margarops fuscatus*), which, due to the lack of trees on the island, has more or less usurped those of the Puerto Ricans. The thrasher is a small but vicious bird, and one biologist reported killing 26 of them which were attempting to drive a single Puerto Rican Amazon from its nest.

Yellow-shouldered Amazon Parrot (*A. barbadensis*)

The scientific name for the yellow-shouldered is based on a mistake, since the word *barbadensis* translates to "of Barbados" and these parrots are not found on Barbados at all. They are found almost exclusively on the island of Aruba, situated just off the coast of Venezuela.

At the turn of the century, this species was reported as very numerous in the wild, though extremely shy and not easily caught due to their limited territory. The bird's rapid demise is linked to the expansion of the oil-refinery business in Venezuela. In 1955, the yellow-shouldered was claimed to be extinct, but two specimens were observed in 1957. Its reduction in numbers through 1930 to 1940 was quite rapid, and by 1948 only a few breeding pairs were thought to be left in existence. This parrot is on the Washington Convention's list of endangered species.

The yellow-shouldered is very similar to the Mexican double yellow-head (*A. ochrocephala oratrix*). It is 13 inches in length. The forehead and lores are a yellowish white. The crown,

Headstudy of a mealy Amazon. This species is considered to be rather loud and is not often seen in captivity.

cheeks and ear-coverts are yellow. The flight feathers are quite dark, ranging from a dark blue to almost black. The eye is a dark orange and the beak a light horn color. The shoulders are a bright yellow.

Imperial Amazon Parrot (*A. imperialis*)

The imperial Amazon parrot is the largest species of the genus *Amazona*. It is 19 to 20 inches in length. From its name alone one would guess that it is a beautiful bird; indeed, the Duke of Bedford, who kept many of the Amazons, called it "the emperor of all true parrots." The head, neck, breast and abdomen are a purplish blue, with black edges to the feathers. The feathers of the crown and the back of the neck are edged with dark green. The primaries and secondaries are dull purple, with green and blue visible. The tail is red to reddish brown. The iris is orange. These parrots are unusual because the hen is considerably larger than the male.

The imperial Amazon is found only in the Lesser Antilles; it is quite possible that this species is already extinct. The imperial has never been seen in large numbers, due not only to its limited territory in the wild but because it lives high up in the mountainous regions, where even the local natives have difficulty spotting it. This parrot is under limited protection in its own country and is not under the Washington Convention's list of endangered species. It was first exhibited by the London Zoo in 1865.

Red-necked Amazon Parrot
(*A. arausiaca*)

The red-necked Amazon Parrot was very common as late as the 1930's, but its numbers have been rapidly depleted by land clearance, shooting and trapping. Its territory consists of a single island, Dominica, in the Caribbean Lesser Antilles. The red- necked is sometimes called the lesser Dominican Amazon and sometimes Bouquest's Amazon.

The forehead, parts of the crown and cheeks are sea blue. The general plumage is green. This parrot is 16 inches in length. The foreneck is red, as are parts of the upper breast. Most of the feathers are edged with black. The iris is orange. The bill is flesh-colored.

Very few specimens of the red-necked have been sent to Europe. The number shown in England numbers no more than six, of which one was shown in the London Zoo in 1900.

Black-billed Jamaican Amazon Parrot (*A. agilis*)

The black-billed Amazon is found on Jamaica. At one

time flocks of twenty or more parrots were common, but its numbers have since dropped to dangerous levels. The black-billed Jamaican was thought to be fewer in number than the imperial Amazon parrot. Rutgers and Norris report that these birds were hunted extensively as pests. They are under limited protection on the island of Jamaica today.

The black-billed Jamaican is a small Amazon and is about 10½ inches in length. Its green plumage is said to be more beautiful than that of any of the other Amazons. The color of the head is a bright shade of green, with a bluish tinge at the top. The beak is grayish black. The feathers of the neck are edged in black. A pale spot is often visible on the upper mandible. The primaries are black to violet- blue; the secondaries are blue. The iris is dark brown.

The red-necked Amazon is a beautifully colored bird with bright, striking plumage.

Yellow-billed Amazon Parrot (*A. collaria*)

A hundred years ago this species was not uncommon in confinement, but today it is very rare. It is on the list of endangered species of the Washington Convention. There is no record of its breeding in captivity. It has a small distribution.

The yellow-billed is a small parrot of rather slender build. It feeds on fruit and the kernels of cashew nuts, berries and leafy foliage. It has been observed nesting in tall trees and in the cavities left by woodpeckers. Natives reportedly often kill the birds for their feathers, particularly the green feathers of the young parrots.

The yellow-billed, also called the red-throated Amazon parrot, has a pinkish red color around the cheeks and throat, extending to the neck. It is 11 1/2 inches in length. The over-all plumage is green, with a brighter green on the breast. As with many other Amazons, the feathers of the crown and neck are edged with black. The flights are darkish blue. The base of the tail is yellow and pink. The bill is a corn color.

This parrot was first acquired by the London Zoo in 1869. This and the black-billed are the two native species of Jamaica. It is found in the forested hills and mountains. A hundred years ago this parrot, like many others, was kept as a cage-bird. Today, though it is not extinct and is even found in some numbers in spots, it is becoming increasingly rare in the wild.

The Duke of Bedford says that this parrot is noisy and a poor talker. Other keepers of the yellow-billed Jamaican seem to agree with the Duke, describing it as dull and not as interesting as the other Amazons. However, it has been bred in captivity.

St. Lucia Amazon Parrot (A. versicolor)

This parrot is well protected in its homeland, and limited numbers of species may again be exported. In any case, laws against the killing and trapping of this parrot are stringently enforced on the island of St. Lucia in the Lesser Antilles. At the turn of the century the St. Lucia was listed as near extinction. Very few bird keepers have ever seen this parrot. Rosemary Low, in her book *The Parrots of South America*, says that the Duke of Bedford had a St. Lucia Amazon, but the bird and the species are not mentioned in the Duke's book, *Parrots and Parrot-Like Birds*. This bird has never been bred in captivity.

The St. Lucia is 16 to 17 inches in length. The color of the plumage is olive-green, with the feathers heavily

With the enforcement of environmental and species protection laws, it is hoped that the endangered birds will strengthen their numbers and become available to more zoos and serious breeders around the world. These birds are Dufresne's Amazons.

marked with black. The upper breast is speckled with red feathers. The beak is dark. The breast is mostly olive green and the lower breast golden olive. Sometimes called the versicolor Amazon parrot.

Mealy Amazon Parrot (A. farinosa)

Although this parrot has a wide distribution (Venezuela, Guyana and most of Brazil), it is not often kept as a pet. Those bird-owners who have kept it report that it is very loud for an Amazon and, additionally, is not brightly colored. The mealy Amazon parrot is found in the lowland forests and the areas around the mouths of rivers, where it likes to bathe. It nests in April and has a clutch of three eggs.

The mealy Amazon is 15 to 16 inches in length. The amount of yellow differs from bird to bird, with more yellow present in the older birds. The primary feathers are black, with suffused blue and green. The general plumage is green. The iris in the immatures is dark brown, turning to red as the bird grows older.

St. Vincent Amazon Parrot (A. guildingii)

This species is found only on the island of St. Vincent in the Lesser Antilles. This parrot has always been rare. A specimen was first exhibited in the London Zoo in 1874. They are reported to be good talkers although not as good as other Amazons like the Mexican double yellow-head.

Although not on the Washington Convention's list of endangered species, the St. Vincent Amazon is in imminent danger of extinction. Under 500 of the birds are believed to be alive on the 130 square-mile island of St. Vincent. Those parrots that have been transferred to zoos have not done well either, and all but three or four have died. The only successful captive breeding to date of a pair of St. Vincents was at the Houston Zoo early in the 1970's.

In the late 1800's the St. Vincent was one of the most popular of the Amazons because of its size and coloration, which are said to be second only to those of the imperial Amazon. The demise of the St. Vincent was

A newly acquired double yellow-headed Amazon parrot. Amazon parrots bite out of fear, not bad temper.

caused by a number of factors. One was a severe hurricane in 1898 that left the surrounding rivers and coastal areas flooded. A volcanic eruption followed immediately afterward, which killed off more parrots as well as destroyed their nesting sites. St. Vincents are slow breeders and never fully recovered from these calamities.

The St. Vincent Amazon is also called Guilding's Amazon parrot. It is 16 to 18 inches in length. The forehead, front of the crown, as well as the area around the eyes, are white. The feathers of the crown are tipped with lilac, as are the cheeks and ear coverts. The iris is orange and the bill is corn-colored. The upper tail coverts are brown. The feathers of the neck are blue and the feathers of the upper breast are brown.

Taming and Training

PARROTS IN THE WILD

People often forget that the parrot, in contrast to the canary or the budgerigar, is basically a wild bird. It is distrustful of man. Although most parrots are eventually tamed, parrots are temperamental. They form intimate likes and dislikes that can be very difficult to change. That is why only one person should be the trainer during training. Another thing that is important is that only a young bird, one that has not yet formed a personality, should be trained.

Before this century, a prospective bird-owner was at a great disadvantage. For one thing, the bird he bought was usually an older bird (in commercial trade a bird that is much over a year old is considered to be "old"). The older bird was chosen because it had a better chance of survival due to the long shipment time. Also, when a young bird was shipped it was often an old bird by the time it was offered for sale. Not only were these parrots difficult to train, but the bird-owner was given little instruction on how to properly train his bird. Some of the taming techniques used were absolutely useless. One technique was to hit the bird if it refused to talk. This did more damage than the trainer could wish because a bird has an instinctual fear of a man's hand. Another trick, in common use, was cutting the bird's tongue in the hopes of increasing its possible vocabulary. This will do nothing.

Another method, still practiced today, is the "shotgun" method, where the owner attempts to teach his new parrot to talk in a week. Properly training a bird takes many months, and you should not be discouraged if it takes six months or longer. The thing to remember is that you are taming an essentially wild bird and, above all else, will have to gain its confidence.

BUYING A PARROT

The first requirement in purchasing a parrot is to be

A hand-tame yellow-crowned Amazon. Before hand-taming an Amazon, it is recommended that the bird become stick-trained first.

familiar with the size and coloration of the parrot itself. Unfortunately, many of the common names for parrots are confusing and there are unscrupulous people willing to take advantage of people's gullibility. One good example is with the African grey, which is a very popular parrot. Sometimes the African grey is mistaken for the Australian roseate cockatoo or Galah (*Eolophus roseicapilla*). Although I have never seen this cockatoo being passed off as an African grey, I have read that it is sometimes sold under the name of the Australian gray parrot. There is no such bird, and the prospective bird-owner should be aware of this discrepancy since the prices of the two birds are different. Both of these birds are about the same size and both are gray and have pink colors on the breast. This is not to say that the roseate cockatoo is not an excellent aviary bird— in fact, of all the cockatoos kept in captivity it may well be the most popular. However, the roseate cockatoo is not as gifted a talker as the African grey and is much more noisy. This example is

not mentioned to discourage prospective bird-owners, but just to show that either the advice of another bird-owner should be utilized or the birds should be purchased only from a reputable pet shop or aviarist.

The next requirement after you have found the parrot you desire is to determine the physical soundness of the bird. The parrot should not be missing any toes, nor should there be any evidence of mites on him. The nostrils should be clear and dry, without a watery discharge. The bird should have an intelligent look and be interested in what is going on. A bird that keeps it eyes closed or has discharges coming from the eyes may be sick. Since most birds have not yet molted, their feathers will look dry and lack sheen. A bird that is sick will slouch on its perch with its feathers puffed up; the bird does this to retain body heat.

Interestingly enough, feather condition has little to do with the purchasing of a bird. According to Bob Novak of Novak's Aviaries, Long Island, the wing feathers and tail feathers are often pulled out by local natives, who later sell them. Also, the wings may be clipped for ease of shipping. Neither of these conditions is critical since the bird will get a new set of feathers when it molts. A bird with its wings clipped may look awkward because it will not be able to balance itself properly. If there is any question, ask the owner or spread the bird's wings yourself.

In an article entitled "Taming Your Parrot" by Terry Clymire in the June-July, 1978 issue of *Bird World, American Aviculturists Gazette*, the author says that the pet shop owner may guarantee the health of the birds he sells. This may not be a widespread practice, but according to Clymire, under the terms of the agreement, if

Cuban Amazons inside a flight. It is much easier to train a singly kept Amazon, as the bird will usually form a strong attachment to any other birds kept in the same environment.

the owner takes his bird to a veterinarian, who in turn finds the bird unfit, it may be returned to the pet shop owner for a refund.

ACCLIMATIZATION

Acclimatization of a bird like the parrot is critical only if the bird-owner later transfers the bird to an aviary. All parrots are quarantined after importation, and most bird importers are very meticulous in their examination of potentially sick birds. Thus, the parrot purchased in a pet shop is usually in very good health.

If a parrot is to be transferred to an aviary, then it should not be introduced for a period of two weeks. This is always a good precaution before introducing it into an aviary full of birds. Also, the bird-keeper will want to gain some familiarity with the bird.

For the parrot that is to be kept alone in a cage, the bird-owner should be sure that the cage is ready for it when it arrives home. The cage should be large enough to accommodate the bird, with space above its head, and at a minimum wide enough for it to flap its wings. The cage should be in an elevated position, free from drafts, and with a room temperature of between 68° and 75°F. Water, seed, grit and perhaps a piece of fruit should be placed inside. The cage should be covered for the first day.

TRAINING

The first requirement of training is to make sure that other family members do not interfere in the process. Nothing makes a bird more skittish than a cluster of unfamiliar faces and sounds. Birds are much more attuned to quick, sudden movements than is generally suspected.

The first step is to open the cage door and stick the hand inside. The parrot may bite or peck at first, since it has an instinctive fear of a man's hand. The hand should never be inserted with the fingers extended, but with the palm face downward. If the bird will not perch the first few times do not be alarmed; moreover, do not force it or tease it. There are cases of a parrot becoming forever suspicious of an individual who teased it. This first lesson should last no more than fifteen or twenty minutes a day. The object is to show the bird that the hand is friendly, something that will need much patience.

The bird-owner will sense when he is making progress. The next step is to get the bird to perch on the hand, and eventually to perch on the hand and be taken outside of its cage. Use a net if the bird flies away. Trying to catch a bird by hand may be disastrous. Parrots are big and bulky and cannot be held like a budgie or canary. Using a net is much simpler and reduces the risk of damaging the bird's wings. A butterfly net will suffice, or a special net can be bought at a pet store. Those purchased in a pet store come in different size meshes and are made of nylon.

If a bird seems reluctant to perch on either a gloved or bare hand, then the owner might try using a wooden perch. The parrot may accept this more readily than the hand. Hold the perch under the bird's breast and gently push it under the bird so that it will be forced to step onto it. The parrot will move away

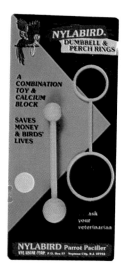

Perch rings are useful tools in trick-training your pet Amazon. Your local pet shop offers different models for different types of birds. Be sure to purchase toys that are made out of safe materials, as are these Nylabird® rings.

several times, but gradually it can be induced to perch on this and later on the hand.

After a bird has learned to perch, it should be taken for a tour of the house. This is to show the bird that its cage is not its only home. If training was done consistently and the bird's confidence gained, it can be placed on a perch that doesn't have wire around it. Many parrots live completely at liberty, and all bird-owners should have this goal in mind when training.

TEACHING TO TALK

Parrots that have been well-trained turn out to be better talkers. Amazons will learn new words all of their lives and will not slow with age. The only real impediment in teaching a bird to talk is the introduction of other birds. If other birds are introduced they become more interested in each other than in learning to talk.

Both male and female Amazons are good talkers. Tales of birds that can recite long phrases and poetry are not exaggerations. Birds, however, do not speak, they mimic. The first few lessons, like the training lessons, should be short, no more than twenty minutes at first. Pronunciation and voice inflection should be regulated so as not to confuse the bird.

The first word to be learned should be short, no more than two syllables. The word should be repeated, with a short pause between each recital. The pause is so the bird will not continually repeat the phrase after it learns it. Do not be surprised if the bird slurs or mispronounces the word on its first try. Keep repeating the word until the bird's pronunciation improves. Reward the bird if it does well.

While the time taken may vary considerably, the main thing is not to get discouraged. I have read of one bird-owner who needed eight months to teach his pet parrot its name.

Getting the bird to respond to a particular phrase is difficult, but not impossible. The bird must be taught a conditioned response: connecting a particular phrase with a particular action or phrase on the part of the owner. One method is to approach the cage, stop and say the phrase, "Fine, thanks." The phrase is repeated until the bird says "Fine, thanks," every time the owner approaches the cage. The owner then says, "How are you?" when he approaches the cage, to which the bird answers "Fine, thanks." Gradually the bird will connect the coming of the owner to the cage and the phrase "How are you?" with the response "Fine, thanks."

TOYS

Toys are really a much needed amusement in the cage, especially for Amazons. Parrots are prone to nervousness and never completely adjust to cage life. The addition of toys provides a diversion for the bird for whom nervousness becomes a neurotic habit sometimes called "displacement preening." Displacement preening is a condition where the bird begins to scratch its head and pick out its feathers to the point of actual injury. The only cure is to provide some diversion.

A yellow-crowned Amazon in the process of becoming stick-trained.

59

Diet

BASIC FOOD REQUIREMENTS

Parrot owners are at an advantage over budgie and canary owners because parrots will eat a variety of foods besides their basic seed mixtures. Parrots will eat corn, a variety of fruits and vegetables, many types of seeds, bread, peanuts and even meat. Most parrots are fussy eaters, but this should not discourage the owner from experimenting.

The basic requirements for a bird are seed, water, cuttlebone and grit. The seed is most important since the bird derives most of its nourishment from this source.

Because of their size, Amazons prefer hefty amounts of larger seed, especially peanuts and sunflower seeds, in their diet.

CANARY SEED

Canary seed comes from canary grass (*Phalaris canariensis*) and, although it grows in wild form, is cultivated in central and southern Europe. It grows to a height of two feet and has bluish leaves. The leaves are elongate like normal grass;

the seed heads are oval or in panicles (loosely branched flower clusters).

With sufficient sunlight the panicles ripen and when collected are thoroughly dried to prevent moldiness. The term Spanish is used to describe top-quality seed. Good seed is fairly large, uniform in size and pale yellow in color. The skin is clean and bright, and when the outer shell is dirty or dull or the inner kernel very light or very dark, then the seed is not of top quality. It may have been badly harvested, insufficiently dried or picked before it was completely ripened.

Canary seed contains the following nutrients: water (13.6%), protein (13.5%), fats and oils (4.9%), starch and other carbohydrates (51.6%) and ash and mineral elements (2.1%).

MILLET SEED

Millet is used basically as a

As they are used to eating a variety of foods in their natural habitat, Amazon parrots are not difficult to feed. Variety and nutrition are most important to the Amazon diet.

filler mixed with other seeds, principally canary. Another use of millet is for exercising the stomach muscles because it has tough fibers. For overweight or underexercised birds, millet is usually given in bigger doses.

Millet is the common name for a wide variety of plants belonging to the genus *Panicum*. Like canary, millet is a grass, of which the most widely used is the plant growing in the tropical arid regions of Africa and the Middle East. This is called white millet (*Panicum miliaceum*). White millet grows to a height of four feet. Its introduction into Europe has resulted in many different varieties, such as black, red, gray and brownish seed.

Another common species of millet is spray millet (*Panicum italicum*), grown in France and Italy. This seed is yellow and smaller than white millet. Spray millet is reserved for smaller birds like finches, lories and lorikeets. Other species of millet are Hungarian millet (*Panicum germanicum*) and Indian millet (*Panicum miliare*).

The nutrient composition of millet is carbohydrate (61.5%), fats and oils (5%), protein (15%), water (13%) and ash and mineral elements (1.6%).

GERMINATING SEED

Seed is germinated as a test of freshness. Differences in commercial preparations can be checked by germinating the seed.

Take a hundred seeds, wet them, place them on a piece of paper and store the paper with the seeds on it in a warm airy place for two or three days. By counting the number of dead seeds the percentage of good seeds in the mixture can be estimated. Obviously, one hundred per cent germination is too much to ask for, but if the count falls below 75-80, you might tell the seller about it. The box of seed may have been on the shelf for too long, or another brand of seed should be selected.

Seed should be purchased in small amounts, no more than two or three pounds per bird. It should be kept in a porous bag and stirred by hand every other day to prevent moldiness.

Some bird-owners prefer to

A vinaceous Amazon enjoying a natural snack. Amazons enjoy greens as well as seed, but green food should not be given too often.

buy quantities of seed and mix their own. A common mixture is four parts canary to two parts millet and one part oats, thoroughly mixed. More oats are added for young birds since oats have a higher percentage of carbohydrates than either canary or millet.

OIL SEEDS

Oil seeds are rich in amino acids, particularly the amino acid lysine, which the non-oil seeds do not have. Since oil seeds are fattening, they are fed only on a weekly basis, either separately or mixed with the regular seed. Common oil seeds used are niger, rape and linseed.

NIGER SEED

Niger seed is grown in northern India and was once

used for lamp oil because of its high oil content. Niger seed (*Guizotia abyssinica*) is closely related to sunflower seed.

Niger seed contains close to 35% oil. When refined, the oil turns from a brown to a pale yellow color. The better the quality of seed the more black and shiny is the husk. Some breeders do not use this seed or only feed it during the breeding season. The reason for this is that niger is more prone than the other oil seeds to turn rancid. Niger seed is a small, long, thin seed and is often squashed during commercial transportation. This spoils the quality of the oil. In commercial mixtures niger is mixed with other oil seeds like rape and linseed.

The nutrient content of niger is water (8.4%), protein (17.5%), fats and oils (32.7%), starches and other carbohydrates (15.3%) and ash and trace elements (7.0%).

RAPE SEED

Rape seed is from a species of cabbage. The types usually encountered are the English and the German. Both are members of the genus *Brassica*, but the German is the one used most often in commercial mixtures. Good rape seed is red to purplish brown in color. Like niger it is small, but is round and less prone than niger to turn rancid during storage.

The nutrient content of rape seed is water (11.5%), protein (19.4%), fats and oils (40.5%), starches and other carbohydrates (10.2%) and ash and mineral matter (3.9%). Rape has an unusually high quantity of phosphoric acid, almost 50 per cent of its ash and mineral content.

LINSEED

Linseed (*Linum usitatissimum*) comes from the flax plant. Flax reaches about two feet in height. The leaves are narrow and usually attain an inch in length. The flowers are blue. Linseed is also fed to race horses along with oats for its oil content. Like all of the oil seeds, linseed must be of good quality. If the oil turns rancid, the seed will pass through the stomach undigested.

Just like people, individual Amazons will have their favorite foods. This blue-fronted Amazon is about to enjoy a peanut.

SPROUTED SEED

Sprouting your own seed is the best way to gain the maximum in freshness and nutritional value; however, the disadvantage is that the sprouted seeds must be used within a few days, before the sprouts grow too large or begin to rot.

Usually a preserving agent is used. One of the more popular ones is calcium propionate. The preserving

Above: *A pair of white-fronted Amazons. The female, seen from the rear, is immature.* **Opposite:** *A lilac-crowned Amazon.*

agent is mixed in with a seed mixture, usually canary, proso millet and oats. The mixture is then germinated by placing it in a bucket that has holes drilled into the bottom and pouring in water to wet the seed. The wet seed is left in the bucket and placed in a warm spot.

Within a day the seed will have germinated and grown sprouts. It is rewatered again every twelve hours until the sprouts have reached a size from one to two inches, when they can be fed to the birds. The process takes about three or four days.

GRIT

Few people realize that commercially prepared grit is crushed granite with minerals such as sulphur, calcium and phosporus added. Grit has little nutritive value but is all-important for the bird to help it digest the tough outer shell and fiber of seed. The bird stores grit in its crop and grinds the seed, much as seed is ground in a mill. In the wild, birds use small pebbles and sand for grit. Cage-birds should be provided with grit every week, whether they use all of the

grit provided or not. Birds will often pass by those particles that are not the right size for them.

For larger aviaries, grit can be purchased in bulk. Most aviary owners add other nutrients to their grit such as crushed egg shell (boiled for twenty minutes to prevent salmonella), crushed oyster shell and other nutrients available at local pet shops.

CUTTLEBONE

The beaks of all birds grow, and the provision of a cuttlebone is to help keep the beak in trim, much as a bone is provided for a dog. All parrots are hard chewers, so the common budgie cuttlebone is too soft. Extra hard cuttlebones are available at local pet shops and should be provided for the pet parrot. The cuttlebone also provides nutrients; it is taken from the cuttlefish and is composed mostly of calcium carbonate.

GREENS

Greens provide vitamins, principally vitamin A for the eyes. They are also important as a source of pigment for keeping up the feather color.

For some parrots which drink very little, like the African grey, the addition of greens serves as an additional source of moisture.

Greens are the easiest of the bird's nutritional requirements to supply since they can be grown at home or purchased in a supermarket. Spinach, endive, chickweed and lettuce are commonly eaten by Amazons. Lettuce contains more nutritional value than is usually ascribed to it.

FRUITS

Amazons will eat a variety of fruits: oranges, apples, melons, etc. The owner needs to remember that a bird's throat is not as large as its mouth. Oranges and apples should be sliced and hung at the side of the cage.

COD-LIVER OIL AND WHEAT GERM OIL

Cod-liver and wheat germ oils are often used by aviary owners as an added source of nutrients. Neither is a must, but because they are oils they might be given as an added source of amino acids. They are not to be mixed into the grit or seed mixture as

Vitamin supplements are nutritious additions to your Amazon's diet. Your local pet shop will offer several brands from which to choose.

they will turn rancid. They should be mixed in a special seed mix that is to be fed to the bird on the day mixed. They might also be used when the birds reach the breeding season to help prevent egg-binding.

Below: *A white-fronted Amazon in an outdoor aviary. Parrots are chewers and often strip the bark from the trees in which they perch.*

Above: *Salle's Amazon, also called Hispaniolan Amazon, in a parrot cage. Light-wired cages which are suitable for budgies or cockatiels are unsatisfactory for Amazons, as the Amazon is larger and may be able to chew through the wire.*

Cage and Aviary

Whether parrots will do better in a cage or an aviary is a matter of dispute.
Undoubtedly a parrot, in fact any bird, will be happier in an aviary setting. Aviaries are roomy and allow flight and the companionship of other birds. If one chooses to breed the bird then an aviary is a better setting. However, the advantages of a cage are many, too. For one thing, a bird that is expected to talk will learn better if left alone in a cage, away from other birds. Additionally, big birds, like macaws, conures and larger parrots, are more amenable to the taming process and frequently can be let out of the cage once they are tamed. In any case, though they do not get the exercise that an aviary can provide, parrots do live

remarkably long and happy lives in cages.

Amazons need a large cage. For all sizes of Amazons a recommended size is three feet in length, two feet in width and two feet high. This may seem unduly large but will more than satisfy the bird's longing to move around. There will be enough head room and room for movement using the dimensions given. Of course smaller cages can be used upon the recommendations of a reliable pet dealer or aviarist.

The most important consideration in the selection of a site for the cage is that it be free from drafts. Amazons live in tropical climates and are very susceptible to colds and diarrhea. The room temperature should be maintained between 65° to 75°F. The cage should be elevated for the bird's comfort, either on a table or suspended from the ceiling. Since the bird will not have any concealment there should not be excessive sunlight. Many people keep their birds in the basement, which is fine if the room is dehumidifed. Also the

circulation of gas or oil fumes should be checked as they are sure to be injurious over a long period of time.

All kinds of cage material are used, from stainless steel to wood, brass and glass.

Most cages made today have a sliding tray on the bottom that greatly facilitates cleaning. The bird rarely has to be removed; the tray is simply pulled out to remove soiled newspaper.

Sometimes the cage bars are painted, which is really a needless task. It is only done by aviary owners who paint their netting to make sure the birds see it and do not fly into it.

THE AVIARY

The aviary is a compound structure that has two sections: the shelter or birdhouse and the flight. The flight is used for exercise. It is a wire enclosure that is usually four or five times larger than the birdhouse. There is a doorway or entrance connecting the two so the birds can fly from the birdhouse into the flight.

The prime considerations in buying or building an aviary are the space available and

A play area will provide your pet Amazon with hours of amusement. Visit your local pet shop to see the various models on the market. Do be sure, however, to purchase a set that is safe and strong enough for your pet, and see to it that the cage or aviary does not become too crowded with toys.

the number of birds to be housed. As to the selection of the birds, the aviarist should always be aware that birds are territorial and some birds are mean towards smaller birds. Also, if the birds are to be bred, then breeding pairs should never occupy the same area or they will fight. The rule for breeding parrots is one pair or three pairs or more, but never two pairs.

The floor of both the birdhouse and the flight is made from either cement or hardwood. Bare earth can be used but, in addition to harboring parasites, it may have to be dug over every few months, limed and returfed. Cement allows the bird-owner to hose down his aviary without worrying about warping or muddying the floor.

The roof of the birdhouse is usually made of shingles, sheet metal or tile. Ventilating ducts are drilled near the roof, which is slanted for rainfall. The ducts are wire-covered to prevent the birds from getting out and predators from getting in. Predation is a major problem with aviaries since mice, weasels, raccoons and stray cats are very adept at crawling under wire or biting through it. One bad night has wiped out more than one aviarist.

Heating may be a radiator or an electric heater. This should be placed in the birdhouse and great care should be taken in the matter of fire safety. The inside of the birdhouse usually has a great deal of hay or foliage for nest-building or for the birds to play with. A fire inside a birdhouse would be a great tragedy.

Netting or wire for the aviary is determined by weight and size of mesh. The smallest mesh for budgies is one-half to three-quarters of an inch mesh. Usually one-inch mesh is used for parrots. This will not keep mice out, but being larger and stronger,

A typical outdoor aviary. This photo was taken at the Jurong Bird Park in Singapore.

A female Australian King parrot. Australian parrots have long tails, while those from South America have shorter tails. Both types, however, require heavy wire mesh for their cages.

will present an obstacle to weasels and raccoons. Usually mesh is painted so the birds will be better able to distinguish it. Lead-free paint, the kind used to paint baby furniture, is the best. As already mentioned, Amazons are chewers and would swallow any chips of paint they could chew away.

Aviary netting and hardware cloth can be ordered through a hardware dealer. Hardware cloth is more expensive than aviary netting but is less brittle.

Most flight sections are made of wire with wooden frames. Sometimes several flight sections are attached to one central birdhouse. A good size of flight for parrots is from 15 to 20 feet, with a height of eight feet. Perches or roosts are placed near the ceiling, since not only do birds like to roost in elevated positions, but when the bird-owner enters he will not have to distract the birds.

The birdhouse is often a converted shed, garage or greenhouse. If you are not a handyman, several types of indoor birdhouses can be purchased, with or without a shelter attached. These indoor birdhouses are usually made of wood with wire to keep the birds from flying away. Sometimes rollers are on the bottom for ease of movement. The small size of these birdhouses prohibits the keeping of more than a single parrot or a breeding pair.

Some bird breeders insist on a small flight section, say of under four feet in length. These breeders have a multitude of young fledglings at any time and, since these birds are inexperienced fliers, they often fly into the wire netting. By decreasing the flying range of the flight the damage a new fledgling can do to itself is greatly diminished. There is nothing wrong with this reasoning, except that it is contradictory. The purpose of the flight is to give the birds exercise room, so generally the larger the flight the better. If possible, such bird breeders should

use two flight sections or netting padded with nylon instead of wire. Another method greatly used is lining the floor of the flight with foliage. Young birds fly not only to test their wings, but, being nervous, to find a place to hide. This method of lining the floor of the flight works especially well with grass parakeets, which are ground-dwellers.

So vast a topic as the building, design and use of an aviary cannot be fully covered by a book of this size. For those who are interested in building an aviary from scratch, the book *Building an Aviary* by Carl Naether and Dr. Matthew M. Vriends is recommended. A lot of time and money goes into building an aviary, and this book will go far toward answering any questions on the topic.

PERCHES

Domesticated birds spend a considerable portion of their lives on their perches, and they are really quite important. Birds sometimes copulate on their perches. Additionally, perches should be of varying thicknesses so that the bird's feet will not become cramped. In the cage, perches are placed so that the bird has enough head room, while in the aviary they are placed near the ceiling for the bird to perch in an elevated position, and spaced far enough apart so that the bird's droppings will not fall into the water dishes or upon the head of another bird.

For Amazon parrots, perches should vary in thickness from two to four inches, depending upon the species kept. Perches that are too small will not be grasped properly by the bird, and if they are too large the bird will not be able to maintain its balance.

Both natural branches and purchased perches can be used.

DRINKING FACILITIES

Amazon parrots, unlike the African grey parrot, love to bathe. If a single parrot is kept in a wire cage, a mixing bowl might be placed inside from time to time as a treat to allow the bird to get its feathers wet. In the aviary Amazons would consider it a great treat if the owner would come by with the hose and

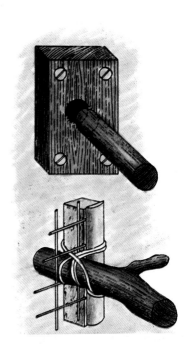

Either commercially made dowels or natural wood branches may be used as perches for your pet Amazon. Natural wood perches offer different diameters, which will aid in keeping the Amazon's feet and claws in good shape. However, when using natural wood perches in the cage or aviary, be sure that they have never been treated with dangerous chemicals.

turn the spray to a fine mist to give them a nice shower. The birds will flap their wings happily and fly around the aviary in a mad rush to get wet. Some bird-owners who have many parrots will install automatic sprinkler systems for the birds' delight on hot, humid days.

The most suitable drinker in an aviary is a Pyrex pie plate or shallow bowl. It should not be so high that the bird has to stand on the lip of the bowl to drink. A crust of algae will form underneath, which should be scraped away with a putty knife. Some aviarists leave the algae and move the plate so the birds will eat the algae. Algae are rich in iodine; however, the birds will most surely step on the growth while eating and that, plus any bacteria that might infest the algae, is good enough reason to scrape it away. Besides, additives like cod-liver oil will provide the iodine that the birds need.

FEEDERS
The selection of the type and number of feeders depends on how many birds are being kept. In a cage, a single bird always has enough feeding compartments to satisfy it. In a larger aviary, parrots may take over feeders from the smaller birds. This problem is

Yellow-lored Amazons from Honduras. The top bird is a youngster.

These feed and water dishes are too large for this Hispaniolan (Salle's) Amazon. A dish must be too small for the bird to stand in.

eliminated by adding enough feeders to go around, but occasionally a single stubborn bird will deny the other birds the right to eat out of spite. In rare cases the bird-owner may have to construct special feeders to cure the bird of this habit.

The size of a feeder should not be so small that the bird exerts itself to feed and not so large that it can stand on the seed as it feeds.

Diseases

Amazons are, on the whole, healthy birds. If they do contract a disease they will not quickly succumb to it, as is the case with the African grey parrot. Added to this is that all parrots are quarantined for a period of thirty days. Most importers are quite concerned with the health of their parrots and generally speaking give them the best possible care during their quarantine period. The parrot that you buy in the pet shop is usually a very healthy bird.

The best advice ever given to the owner of a sick bird is to take it to a veterinarian immediately. This is especially pertinent for the aviary owner, where a contagious disease could wipe out his stock of exotic birds. Even if the bird dies overnight it should be taken to a veterinarian, who will do a post-mortem on the bird to discover the reason it died. This is sometimes called "posting."

The subject of bird diseases is a large one. The purpose of this chapter is to identify some of the more common bird ailments along with recommended care. As a more complete reference see *Bird Diseases* by L. Arnall and I.F. Keymer.

IDENTIFYING A SICK BIRD

Sick birds are not so easily identified. In the case of Amazons, a bird may be healthy one day and dead the next. There are some general symptoms, however, which usually take the form of a change of habits. They may refuse to fly and sit in a corner of the cage. Another common symptom is that the bird has its feathers fluffed up. This is a sign that the bird is trying to retain its body heat by using dead air spaces under its feathers as insulation.

Runny droppings may indicate illness or they may not indicate illness at all, since they may be caused by a change in diet. Diarrhea is not a disease but a symptom, and the bird should be removed to a hospital cage to see if the condition will clear up.

A healthy Amazon should have clear eyes, clean plumage, and an active interest in its surroundings.

An example of a cage well suited to Amazons. The occupant here is a Scaly-headed Parrot.

Dr. Matthew Vriends demonstrates the proper way to hold a small parrot in order to clip its nails.

Other general symptoms are: irregular breathing; the tail jerking up and down; and eyes that are continually closed or discharging fluid.

Any of the mentioned symptoms indicate a bird that is sick, and it should be immediately removed to a hospital cage and taken to a veterinarian as soon as possible.

COLDS

Colds are the most common ailment which a bird will get. They are caused by viruses and are similar to the colds humans catch. The symptoms for a cold are runny nose, sneezing and coughing. While a cold itself is not so serious, left unattended it may develop into pneumonia.

The bird should be removed to a hospital cage with a temperature setting of 95°F. If the eyes are running, epsom salts added to mineral water should be offered.

DIARRHEA

Diarrhea can be a symptom of many diseases. At the same time, diarrhea can persist for a long time without any other effects. Diarrhea is really the result of an inflammation of the intestines

or cloaca with the secretion of an abnormal amount of fluid in the droppings, which become soft and watery. Because of the acid nature of the droppings the tissues surrounding the vent become inflamed.

Placing the bird in a hospital cage is not necessary, since the bird, unless it has contracted a major disease, has no fever. If the condition does not clear up, the bird should be taken to a veterinarian. Check to see if a change in diet has not caused this condition.

It is often stated that green food should be discontinued; in fact some authorities have stated that if the bird's droppings contain blood, it may be caused by greens.

In any case, if persistent, diarrhea may indicate a variety of ailments: a tumor in the kidney, liver damage, inflammation of the urinary tract and a variety of bacterial infections.

PREMATURE MOLT

Premature molt is not strictly speaking a disease; it is a nervous habit, often called displacement preening. Its symptoms are an excessive

Artist's rendering of a typical hospital cage set-up. For a parrot, the hospital cage should be approximately 15 inches high by 12 inches wide by eight inches deep. These cages may be made of metal or wood, and they usually have a sliding glass door. The inside may be insulated with cloth to help maintain heat. A common household light bulb or a special infrared lamp may be used. The temperature inside the hospital cage may range from 80° to 110° F.

picking of the feathers by the bird and scratching the head and feet to excess. In premature molt the bird will do this to such a degree that healthy feathers will be pulled out, leaving bald patches.

Since premature molt is not a disease but a nervous habit, it is difficult to diagnose. For one thing, all birds preen and, in the case of parrots, preening is quite vigorous. Also, birds molt at least once a year (every 8 months for Amazons) and it is normal for them to scratch excessively as the new pinfeathers break the surface of the skin.

Premature molt is rarely lethal, but in extreme cases, where the bird is picking itself bald, there is really no cure. It is caused by the bird's isolation and ill-feelings over confinement. Perhaps the best treatment is to install toys inside the cage in the hope that the bird will occupy itself with these rather than pick at its feathers.

BROKEN LIMBS
Broken wings are common enough and merely need to be set. In some cases the wing will have to be removed. This should be done by a veterinarian since he will be using a sterilized instrument. Some birdmen can set the limb using a match or blade of wood, but this requires experience, since if improperly set it will not heal correctly. The wing is set in a flexed position, and the owner should provide perches near the ground for these birds.

A broken leg should also be set by a veterinarian. Properly set the bird will not be immobilized.

MITES
So many kinds of mites attack birds that it is difficult to find a comprehensive list and treatment. Mites attack the feathers, the skin, the air sacs, the feet, etc. This section will be concerned with two mites: one that causes scaly-leg and a common blood-sucking mite known as the red mite.

Scaly-leg is caused by a very tiny mite that bores under the scales of the feet and lives on the connective tissue. Scaly-leg can be diagnosed in birds whose feet have unduly large scales a consequently dirty appearance to the legs. The

Above left: *Orange-winged Amazon.* **Above right:** *White-fronted Amazon.* **Below left:** *Blue mutation of the Panama Amazon on exhibit in a zoo in Holland.* **Below right:** *Cuban Amazon.*

mite that causes this ailment is less than 1/200th of an inch long and almost impossible to see without the aid of a magnifying glass.

The introduction of this mite into an aviary is caused by using unclean perches, failing to wash the perches when they become dirty or introducing birds into the aviary without washing their feet.

The cure is simple enough. First, all the perches should be cleaned. Then the bird's feet should be washed with olive oil to soften the scaly appearance. After a few days these scales can be taken off without harm and the tissue underneath anointed with either olive oil or petroleum jelly. The oil or jelly will suffocate the mites.

The red mite (*Dermanyssus*) is seen quite frequently. It is a small tick-like creature which measures about $1/75$ to $1/100$th of an inch in length. By gently separating the bird's feathers, these mites can be spotted.

The red mite gets its name because, being a blood-sucker at night, it will be gorged with blood the following day and if crushed will become a red splotch from the blood. Red mites attack only at night and during the day seek some shelter to hide in, usually the cracks of the perches, nests and the aviary. Among breeders, they can become so numerous as to drive the hen from her nest and bleed the young chicks to death.

Since red mites leave the birds during the day, they can be spotted and killed. The general remedy is to completely cleanse the aviary, washing or even replacing the perches, and washing and spraying with a safe insecticide the rest of the aviary. Straw used in nest-boxes should be removed.

TAPEWORMS

Contrary to popular belief, there are quite a few species of tapeworms. There are at least nine species of tapeworms that attack chickens and turkeys. Diagnosis is that the feces will contain worm segments in the droppings; the droppings are at first watery, but later brownish yellow due to bleeding.

A green-cheeked or Mexican red-headed Amazon.

An infestation of tapeworms in a well-run aviary is rare, because it requires an infected bird getting into the aviary. Tapeworms attach themselves to the mucous membranes of the intestines and release their eggs into the feces of the bird; if these feces are digested by another bird then that bird will become infected.

Tapeworms luckily are rarely fatal, and once diagnosed there are a number of medications that will wipe them out.

ROUNDWORMS
Like tapeworms, there are many varieties of roundworms. They range in size according to the size of the bird. Those found in canaries are from one-quarter to three- quarters of an inch long.

These worms are passed on through the feces and through the food. They are very dangerous since they multiply to such numbers that they may block the intestines and kill the bird. They can be diagnosed in the feces, but only under a microscope. The best cure is prevention: keep the cage clean on a regular basis.

Breeding

Breeding Amazons in captivity is rare. These parrots are very temperamental and essentially wild birds. Additionally, the price of a breeding pair is a big investment involving hundreds of dollars. Finally, after finding a true pair the time and patience required may total many years. Amazons are usually sold under a year of age and the hens are not ready to mate until three years of age.

The purpose of this chapter is to familiarize prospective breeders with some of the problems involved in breeding parrots.

SEXING

Unfortunately, there is no 100 per cent fool-proof method of sexing birds using sight alone.

Clues as to the sex of the bird are few. Generally, however, the male is larger than the female and more brightly colored. The head and the beak of the male are noticeably larger. The shape of the eyes is different: the female's are smaller and elliptical in shape, while the male's are more round.

Another possible clue is feeling the pelvic bones. The male's pelvic bones are closer together than the female's, because she must pass eggs. Obviously it takes a great deal of familiarity with the species of parrot to make a good guess as to the sex of the bird.

Sexing is critical for breeding, and recently a method has been introduced to determine sex by performing a minor operation on the prospective birds to be bred. A small incision is made in the stomach area. This will not damage the female's ovaries or interfere with the male's sexual reproduction. An operation might seem like an exaggerated way to determine sex, but it isn't, considering the difficulty in accurately determining the sex of a bird.

COURTSHIP AND NESTING

The nesting habits of Amazons have rarely been observed or described. In captivity, it has been observed that the female takes the lead in courtship and at the onset of breeding will dance around the cock

Yellow-naped Amazon.

with wings held low and tail spread out. The male, too, may engage in dancing with the feathers displayed. Sometimes, the pupil of the eye dilates. The cock may strut and climb about the wire. A distinguishing factor of psittacine males is that when they mount the female they always place both feet on the back. Just before copulation there will be considerable body contact, according to Forshaw in his book *Parrots of the World*.

Parrots are notorious for their lack of selection of a suitable nesting site in the aviary. Often the hen will lay her eggs on the floor of the cage and incubate them there. She will become distraught if any attempts are made to induce her to incubate her eggs in a nest-box.

For breeding purposes a nest-box should be placed in the cage. It should be made of sturdy wood and lined with a smaller layer of peat. Since Amazons prefer tree hollows, the inside of the nest-box should not allow much light inside and should not be too spacious. Once the hen lays, the nest should not be disturbed. Incubation is approximately 28 days. The male will feed the female, who in turn will feed the young regurgitated food.

Egg problems are usually associated with deficiencies of grit and greens in the diet. The formation of the egg shell in the hen is greatly dependent on the diet of the bird. The shell must be of porous nature, to allow oxygen and carbon dioxide to pass freely to the developing embryo, and also hard enough to serve as a layer of protection. Deficiencies of calcium are responsible for egg-binding and soft-shelled eggs.

Egg-bound is a condition whereby the hen is unable to expel her eggs; they become stuck in the pelvic area, and if not removed both hen and egg will die. The hen will usually try vainly to expel the egg and paralysis may occur. This condition can be diagnosed by feeling for the egg in the stomach region.

Egg-binding is often associated with a lack of calcium, but the condition may occur in old hens. Some bird-owners can free the egg by inserting a well oiled finger into the cloaca and up into the oviduct. By gentle pressure with the free hand on the stomach they can expel the egg. This is a delicate operation, for if the egg breaks the hen may die. If the bird is to be saved at all, however, action must be taken very soon after the condition is diagnosed, otherwise the bird will die. A soft-shelled egg is usually caused by a calcium deficiency.

Index

AMAZON PARROTS
KW-012